FIRST DAY OF SCHOOL

Billy Aronson

BROADWAY PLAY PUBLISHING INC
New York
www.broadwayplaypublishing.com
info@broadwayplaypublishing.com

First printing: December 2010
Second printing: March 2011
I S B N: 978-0-88145-480-2

Book design: Marie Donovan
Page make-up: Adobe Indesign
Typeface: Palatino
Printed and bound in the U S A

ABOUT THE AUTHOR

Billy Aronson's plays have been produced by
Ensemble Studio Theater, Playwrights Horizons,
Woolly Mammoth Theater, Wellfleet Harbor
Actors Theater, 1812 Productions, Amphibian Stage
Productions, City Lights Theater Company, and the
S F Playhouse; awarded a commission from the Magic
Theater, a grant from the New York Foundation for the
Arts, and an Outstanding Original Script prize from
the Bay Area Theater Critics Circle; and published in
5 volumes of Best American Short Plays. His writing
for the musical theater includes the original concept/
additional lyrics for the Broadway musical RENT,
and the book for the Theaterworks/U S A musical
CLICK CLACK MOO, which received a Lucille Lortel
nomination for Best Musical. His TV writing credits
include M T V's *Beavis & Butt-head* , Cartoon Network's
Courage the Cowardly Dog, and Nickelodeon's *Wonder
Pets*, for which he served as head writer and received
an Emmy Award. He lives in Brooklyn with his
wife Lisa Vogel and their children Jake and Anna.
("billyaronson.com")

FIRST DAY OF SCHOOL was originally produced by 1812 Productions, Philadelphia, Pennsylvania (Jennifer Childs, Artistic Director; Kate Tejada, Managing Director), and S F Playhouse, San Francisco, California (Bill English, Artistic Director; Susi Damilano, Producing Director).

The Philadelphia production opened on 7 October 2009. The cast and creatives contributors were:

SUSAN	Karen Peakes
DAVID	Pete Pryor
PETER	Chris Faith
KIM	Susan Riley Stevens
ALICE	Jennifer Childs
BELINDA	Eileen Cella
JONAH	Michael Tomasetti
Director	Pete Pryor
Associate director	Matt Pfeiffer
Dramaturg	Elizabeth Pool
Set design	Dirk Durossette
Costume design	Alisa Sickora Kleckner
Lighting design	Paul Moffitt
Sound design	Chris Colucci
Production stage manager	Thomas E Shotkin

The San Francisco production opened on 26 September 2009. The cast and creative contributors were:

SUSAN	Zehra Berkman
DAVID	Bill English
PETER	Jackson Davis
KIM	Marcia Pizzo
ALICE	Stacy Ross
BELINDA	Torie Laher
JONAH	Myles Landberg
Director	Chris Smith
Set design	Bill English
Costume design	Bree Hylkema
Lighting design	Cy Eaton
Sound design	Matt Stines
Production stage manager	Nicola Rossini

The play was subsequently produced by Amphibian Stage Productions, Fort Worth, Texas (Kathleen Anderson Culebro, Artistic Director; Rebecca Allard, Managing Director), where it opened on 8 July 2010. The cast and creative contributors were:

SUSAN ....Molly Lloyd
DAVID .... Patrick Bynane
PETER .... Marshall York
KIM... Krista Scott
ALICE .... Desiree Fultz
BELINDA ....Sydney Baumgart
JONAH...Alex Bush

Director ....Evan Mueller
Set design ....Kathleen Culebro & Alix Milne
Costume design ....Aaron Patrick Turner
Lighting design ....Chad R Jung
Sound design...David Lanza
Production stage manager ....Lisa Marie Lange

It was then produced by City Lights Theater Company, San Jose, California (Lisa Mallette, Executive Artistic Director; Kit Wilder, Associate Artistic Director, Production Manager), where it opened on 23 September 2010. The cast and creative contributors were:

SUSAN .... Diahanna Davidson
DAVID .... Tom Gough
PETER .... Rich Miller
KIM.. Mandy Manousos
ALICE .... Courtney Walsh
BELINDA .... Rachel Wilde
JONAH... Shane Rhoades

Director .... Virginia Drake
Set design .... Ron Gasparinetti
Costume design .... Amy Conners
Lighting design .... Jim Gross
Sound design .... Rich Miller
Prop design .... Kacey Kvamme
Production stage manager .... Gilly Kelleher

ACKNOWLEDGEMENTS

During its development, FIRST DAY OF SCHOOL was presented in readings by Playwrights Horizons, the Magic Theatre/Z Space Studios New Works Initiative, the National New Play Network, Ensemble Studio Theatre, the SF Playhouse, and 1812 Productions. Thanks to Robert Davenport, David Dower, Chris Smith, Mark Routhier, Sonya Sobieski, Tim Sanford, William Carden, Linsay Firman, Laura Salvato, Casey Stangl, and all of the actors who took part in these readings, for their contributions to the development of the play. And a special thanks to everyone involved in the simultaneous world premieres at 1812 Productions and S F Playhouse, for bringing the play to life.

CHARACTERS & SETTING:

DAVID, *married parent*
SUSAN, *married parent*
PETER, *married parent*
KIM, *married parent*
ALICE, *married parent*
BELINDA, *teenager*
JONAH, *teenager*

Scene 1 takes place outside an elementary school, on the morning of the first day of school.

Scene 2 takes place in the living room of SUSAN *and* DAVID's *home, shortly after.*

Scene 3 takes place in the same living room, 4 years later.

Scene 1

*(*Susan *and* David *stand outside an elementary school)*

David: Miss Rhiner?

Susan: She's the new one, from teacher's college.

David: I thought Tessie was going to have Claire Johnson.

Susan: That's what we heard. But everybody wanted Claire Johnson so they had to switch some kids to Rhiner, but she seems really great.

David: Really?

Susan: She took Tessie by the hand, she said you must be Tessie, she led her right to the activity table.

David: How'd she know her name?

Susan: I have no idea, but she spoke softly, right to Tessie, and it worked like a charm.

David: That's great that Tessie let you go so soon.

Susan: I think we struck gold, honey.

David: Yeah?

Susan: Sure Claire Johnson's beautiful and she plays guitar and has this beautiful voice and Miss Rhiner is kind of plain and quiet but she really has a way with the kids that's sort of amazing. Within about two minutes she had Tessie right in the mix of things, I looked over and she was setting up a plastic food restaurant with three other kids, one of them was Carey Berman.

DAVID: Carey from play group?

SUSAN: Carey's in her class and Nessa from around the block and Katie Baldini-Wertz.

DAVID: Katie's a good kid.

SUSAN: Her moms were there. Harriet and Adina. They want to have us over.

DAVID: I can't believe Tessie let you go just like that.

SUSAN: I think we lucked out. So how's Sam?

DAVID: Misses Bamara seems great.

SUSAN: Oh great.

DAVID: Well she comes off aloof and cool at first and she's definitely not chatty, but she's confident, you know?, she's been there for five years so she doesn't waste words, she's really got it down so the kids can sit back and relax and really listen and contribute.

SUSAN: They say she's not so strong with science but she's great with writing skills which is everything in third grade.

DAVID: Hey Jeff Kunken's in the class.

SUSAN: That's three years in a row for those guys. I'll have to call Marilyn.

DAVID: And Ajami and Simon from last year.

SUSAN: Ajami. Good.

DAVID: And that kid from first grade, Rory Kessler-Something.

SUSAN: Sam's friends Malcolm and Cleo got Mister McClellan who everybody wanted but I guess Sam's good with Bamara.

DAVID: I know he's good because he ignored me.

SUSAN: That's Sam for you.

DAVID: Wouldn't even look over.

SUSAN: He's in his element with Jeff Kunken and Ajami.

DAVID: He's great and Tessie's totally fine.

SUSAN: Both the kids are in school.

DAVID: How about that.

SUSAN: Wow.

DAVID: I know.

SUSAN: This is quite a moment. *(Pause)* It's too bad they cancelled the bagel breakfast. I always love catching up with everybody.

DAVID: They cancelled it 'cause of the budget cuts?

SUSAN: They had less than they realized all of a sudden so they couldn't justify it.

DAVID: If only they'd realized sooner we could have all brought stuff in.

SUSAN: I know.

DAVID: So will you go in to work?

SUSAN: I really want Ellen to get used to handling things. The deal is I'm down to half time. I want to stick with that.

DAVID: I filled out so many forms to get today off, you know the city bureaucracy, once the forms have gone through I couldn't get the day back if I tried.

SUSAN: So we're both completely free.

DAVID: When was the last time that happened.

SUSAN: I went grocery shopping last night so that's done.

DAVID: I think I'll start putting up the bookshelves.

SUSAN: Oh don't, because if you start now there'll be a big mess all over the den this weekend for my sister.

DAVID: Your sister.

SUSAN: They're coming by Saturday to give us our anniversary present in person.

DAVID: Oh right.

SUSAN: She feels bad they couldn't make the party, they want to take us all out to lunch, and also at some point she and I have to talk about nursing homes for dad.

DAVID: Well maybe I'll head to the butcher, I was going to pick up pork chops.

SUSAN: You can do that later. We have this one chance, let's do something really special, like see the Egyptian tombs.

DAVID: I think that was just at the museum for the summer.

SUSAN: You're right. We blew it.

DAVID: We could get out the bikes. Or go to a movie. Or we could try having sex with other people. Or hey, did you want to look at dryers?

SUSAN: I know I complained about the dryer but it's working again so let's wait. Is there a movie you want to see?

DAVID: That thing about the soccer is supposed to be funny. What's her name is in it. Not Julia Roberts, the one who was in, you know.

SUSAN: The kids want to see that, let's wait and see it with them.

DAVID: Sandra Bullock.

SUSAN: We might go biking with my sister, I think they're bringing theirs.

DAVID: That'll be fun.

SUSAN: Maybe we should try having sex with other people.

DAVID: We'd talked about that.

SUSAN: If not now, when.

DAVID: Did you have anybody in mind?

SUSAN: Gosh, let's see, I saw Peter Hanson dropping off Chelsea.

DAVID: He was one of the nicest parents from play-group.

SUSAN: He's really fun to talk to and creative and friendly and he's got a great backside, I'd love to snuggle up against him.

DAVID: Well there you go. Hey was Maxine there too? She's got that deep voice, I really like that.

SUSAN: She had to dash off to work.

DAVID: Darn. Oh, I saw Kim Keeler dropping off the twins. She's really lively and she's in great shape.

SUSAN: Kim would be great, she has so much spirit.

DAVID: I'd really like to see her naked breasts up close and touch them.

SUSAN: You guys would be great, but I wonder if she's still around. Belinda's starting middle school today.

DAVID: Maybe her husband dropped off Belinda, what's his name, Carl.

SUSAN: Carl.

DAVID: Hey there's Peter Hanson. Go get him. I'll try to find Kim. See ya, Sooz.

SUSAN: Have fun, honey.

(DAVID and SUSAN kiss. He starts off.)

SUSAN: Oh David. If you do pass the butcher we could use milk.

DAVID: One percent is it? Or two percent.

SUSAN: One percent.

DAVID: One percent.

(DAVID *goes.*)

SUSAN: Hey Peter.

(PETER *enters.*)

PETER: Hey Susan. Did I see you dropping off Tessie with the new teacher?

SUSAN: Miss Rhiner, she seems great, we're so relieved.

PETER: Oh that's great.

SUSAN: And Chelsea's got Himmelman?

PETER: We're relieved too.

SUSAN: So Himmelman's okay?

PETER: We hadn't heard good things, and I can see why she gets a bad rap. Her face is sort of stern and in the hallway she comes off as gruff, but in the class room she lets down her guard and tells great stories. She's got a great speaking voice and wonderful facial expressions and big gestures, she takes out all these old pictures she's saved up over the years and totally draws the kids in, Chelsea was really enthralled. She gave me a big hug and said go now daddy.

SUSAN: It's funny, the only kindergarten teacher anybody talks about is Claire Johnson but the others are turning out great.

PETER: That's great that Miss Rhiner is good.

SUSAN: I thought she was super. Say do you want to have sex with me?

PETER: Oh gosh. Huh?

SUSAN: Do you want to go back to my house and have sex with me?

PETER: Oh I'm so sorry. I couldn't.

SUSAN: So how are things with Maxine. Her boss at the hospital was giving her trouble.

PETER: They moved him up and out so she's doing fine now except that she's working her tail off. How's your work?

SUSAN: For two years I've been trying to get down to half time without our little practice falling apart and it looks like I finally have the right coverage so it's really going to work out.

PETER: Hey good.

SUSAN: When I was working full time the cost of coverage for the kids was a really sizable chunk of what I was bringing in after taxes so what's the point, you know? We'll never get these years back so why not spend the extra time with the kids.

PETER: Really.

SUSAN: And your painting is going okay? I'm sorry we missed your show last spring. David's mom was in and out of the hospital, he had to keep flying across the country.

PETER: That's okay. I'm having another one in December.

SUSAN: Definitely send us a card.

PETER: Hey I really appreciate what you said before, about, you know. It's just, I can't. It's a question of, you know. But I appreciate it. I really do. I think you're a terrific person. I admire your spirit, and your friendliness, and your eyes, they're just wonderful. You're a very wonderful person and that means so much nowadays. It's just the old thing that we live

under. And I'm not saying it's bad, what you were
suggesting, it's completely natural. I just couldn't
handle, you know, the lying or whatever, Maxine and
I tell each other everything, well not everything, if
there's a surprise party for her obviously I don't tell
her that but that's obviously different, or when I went
out to get her those little thingies that she wanted, the
earrings, I told her I was going out with this friend of
mine Rob and that was a lie, let's call it what it was it
was a lie so we do lie and that's fine, she completely
accepts that we lie, everyone does in a sense, but to be
carrying around a secret, a big big secret, like when
she introduced me to this friend of hers she didn't tell
me that they'd slept together in college until after like
the fourth time we saw him so there I was socializing
with this guy who she'd gone out with in college, or it
was high school, Sasha was his name, Sasha Mallone,
she'd totally concealed their past because she knew
it would make me uncomfortable, she had this secret
but so what. Yes we're married, we're married but
we have thoughts, I don't know what she's thinking,
we can't tell every thought, we're individuals, right?,
we have a bond, but we still you know, we have
separate brains and separate lungs, we're not Siamese
twins, we need to breath on our own like that time
she gave my brother a massage, right in front of the
fireplace, she goes right over to my brother, gives him
a massage, I'm sitting there adding kindling like an
idiot, nobody's massaging me but she massages him,
and I was happy for them both, but I guess I know
this thing you're talking about would be different,
it's more, you know, what's the word, I can't think
of the word, but it's definitely different and I'm only
sorry because it'll mean I won't have a chance to get
to know you in that way and it really limits, doesn't
it, the way we can know each other, it's a shame that
a budding friendship should be cut off like that and

yes sometimes a friendship does sort of veer from
one category into another and then it veers right back
again, it swerves kind of, so we might have had a
wonderfully swerving friendship and to just cut it off,
to limit the possibility for joy in our limited time on
earth, it seems a damn shame to cut off an opportunity
like that, it's pathetic, that's all, to butcher a blossoming
friendship with someone so obviously warm and
outgoing with such beautiful arms and a smile and
great hair and a great smell I mean why can't I just put
my face in your hair and sniff it, you know?, why am I
stuck standing here on the other side of some invisible
divide, this boundary, where is it?, is it here, is it here?,
this ridiculous wall that separates me from someone
with such honesty and openness and the courage to be
direct, such guts, such heart, such warmth, why do we
have to limit ourselves like that?, what's the purpose?,
what's the logic, it's not logical. We're animals. We
live. We have arms. So what.

SUSAN: Anyway.

PETER: And of course we have children, we have kids,
yes, so the bond between the caregivers becomes
crucial, you can't drop the ball, not for a second, we
would never want to burden our children with the
confusion and pain of sensing a parent was limiting
himself, kids are sensitive, they can sense things, they
sense tension, and repression, they do, do we want
to do that to our kids?, to burden them with that?, or
wouldn't we rather give them a model of someone
taking their lives into their hands and ignoring some
inane conventions, some arbitrary whatever, the ages
of nonsense, you know?, wouldn't it be better to stand
up and let them see someone reaching for something
bold, let them see the honest expression, well we
couldn't let them see, it would be very delicately
concealed honest expression but they'd sense it,

the behind-the-scenes bravery, the faithfulness to
nature, the natural faithfully honest expression and
they'd know deep down that the people who cared
for them were living lives of courageous fulfillment
so that when they grew up they wouldn't get to this
point where they're on the threshold of something
great but for some unforeseen reason out of nowhere
they suddenly cut themselves off from their dreams
out of ridiculous guilt and start running like crazy
from their actual desires until after eleven different
kinds of therapeutic unearthing they're able to allow
themselves to enjoy a real life that's full of meaning
and beauty and purpose and freedom and hope.

SUSAN: So you—

PETER: Can't. No. Sorry. I'm, rrrr. What can I say. I
can't, I can't, I'm sorry it's just not me, it's not me, and
I'm so sorry it's not me, I wish it was me, I wish it was
me, I wish it, I do, because it could have been so, you
know, but we have to let it go, and I'm sorry because
I really do think you're special and imaginative and
ravishing with the air from your pores on my flesh but
unfortunately for us both I'm not the kind of person
who can just rip off our clothes and grab each other
and taste I want to taste you, shit. Shit. Shit. Shit. Shit
shit shit shit shit.

SUSAN: So say hi to Maxine for me.

PETER: Listen. I'm touched. By what you said. But
when I die, you understand, and we're all going to
die, I want to know, call it ridiculous, to know I could
say, when I'm lying there twitching, to know I could
look up and say from my soul, uh, d'you want to get a
bagel?

SUSAN: You want to get a bagel?

PETER: I was going to have a bagel with two hundred
people but the breakfast was cancelled and I still want

a bagel so I'm having a bagel with one person, what's wrong with that? What? What?

SUSAN: I guess we—

PETER: No I can't because, as we sat there, there would be, some...thing, in the air, hanging over our every—

(PETER's cell phone rings, he answers it.)

PETER: Oh hi. Great. Yeah she hugged me and said daddy go now. Totally. Yeah. Well it was cancelled but I ran into Susan Tessie's mom and we're getting bagels at the diner. Sure thing. Love you. Bye. *(He hangs it up.)* Whoa. *(Beat)* Let's go get a bagel.

SUSAN: Okay.

(PETER and SUSAN start off together.)

PETER: Maxine says hi.

(As PETER and SUSAN exit, DAVID enters talking to KIM.)

DAVID: And Belinda's starting middle school?

KIM: It feels huge, it's enormous.

DAVID: Gosh Kim.

KIM: And so loud and crazy. The kids are like teenagers.

DAVID: It's a crazy time, right? Especially for a girl.

KIM: There are all kinds of wild emotions and pressures, but she's got so many good friends in her homeroom.

DAVID: That's great she let you walk her to homeroom, Sam barely let me take him to third grade.

KIM: Well no you're right, when we're within like a mile radius of the school I can't look at her let alone talk or god forbid laugh, so I didn't get anywhere near her classroom but I did check the list in the front office and she has three great friends in her class.

DAVID: Oh good.

KIM: It's so important to have old friends around she can trust and rely on, at this kind of transition.

DAVID: Sure.

KIM: Plus I know the guidance counselor, she's terrific, and it turns out Belinda's science teacher went to college with Carl so we have that connection.

DAVID: How is Carl?

KIM: He just signed Kiley from American Idol, she was in the top thirty on the second season and they're getting a ton of work doing commercials for these podcasts and all kinds of internet stuff.

DAVID: Oh yeah?

KIM: So he's been insane in a good way and I've been busy with all this P T A business, it kept me running around all summer so now that school's starting up you can imagine.

DAVID: You're the treasurer, right?

KIM: We're raising money to build up the music program into a real music program and it looks like it's actually possible.

DAVID: That would be great.

KIM: It would take a lot of parent involvement, as always, and fundraising's gotten so much tougher, you have to be really creative.

DAVID: I can imagine. Yeah.

KIM: And don't you know when I dropped by the middle school they want me to get involved there.

DAVID: They've heard about you.

KIM: They really respect what the P T A here has done and they're trying to redo the middle school auditorium.

DAVID: Sure.

KIM: So how are things going with the city?

DAVID: Oh really good, thanks. Do you want to have sex with me?

KIM: Do I what?

DAVID: Do you want to have sex with me?

KIM: Do I want to have sex with you?

DAVID: Yeah.

KIM: Do I want to have sex with you?

DAVID: I was wondering.

KIM: Oh David. How can you ask me that? I have a husband and three children. And you have a wife and kids. What are you thinking? You seriously would just run off and do that, just like that?

DAVID: Yeah.

KIM: My god, maybe I'm naïve but I like to think that people are really with who they say they're with. I made a commitment, I'm sorry, and you made a commitment too David. When you say you're going to be with someone you should stick with them and make it work out. Yes I ran around when I was young, and that was a good time sometimes, I certainly had my good times like anybody else but you made a promise to stay with someone and you need to honor that. And sure, there are problems, there are always going to be problems. So you get counseling. You don't just chuck it for whatever's fun. And I don't even mean fun because how can it be fun sneaking around like that, ducking off somewhere. How can you even conceive of doing that, David? Where would you even go?

DAVID: We could go to my house.

KIM: "We could go to my house." David. "We could
go to my house." Do you hear how filthy that sounds?
We'd just run off to your house. In the middle of
the day. An empty house in the middle of the day,
lounging around naked. How awful does that sound
David, how disgusting. I've got a list of school supplies
to buy for the twins. I was going to try to catch up with
the vice principal about music in the schools and the
pumpkin drive, and I'm sorry if that sounds stupid
to you David but I'd rather be getting something
accomplished than sneaking off to your house in the
middle of the day, like the neighbors wouldn't notice,
and talk, they would talk, or would you have me show
up later? Is that what you're thinking? You'd go in and
then I'd walk in separately a little later? And if anyone
noticed you'd have what?, some kind of story to tell
them? Is that it? You'd say we were talking about the
music program, how some city fundraising program
that you knew from your work could be a model for
the drive I'm planning this coming October? Fine,
so you'd pile one lie on top of another as you snuck
around, risking causing enormous pain for these
wonderful people you love and promised to honor all
your life and for what David. What. Three minutes of
pleasure? Ten minutes? Half an hour?

DAVID: I'm free until school lets out.

KIM: Five hours of pleasure. Fine. Five hours of
incredible bliss. Hooray. Let's hear it for David with
his five hours of rolling around naked and squashing
your thighs together and feeling each other up and
squealing like animals, well okay Mister Five Hours,
you know what I say? I say big deal David it's still just
fun, that's all it is, a little fun. Oh David, I'm sorry but
men are just hard-wired different than women, I'm
not interested in jumping into bed with somebody,
that's not how my mind works, I don't think about

sex every three seconds and I'm not led around by my lap, but don't stand there staring at me like I'm this passionless whatever because of course I have feelings, I have impulses, everyone has their whimsical you know desires but I don't let them drag me around like a dog, I use them to help me do better, okay David?, I channel my desires to make me a better person, a stronger person, yes I do David, you can't give in to every little temptation for god sake, go for a jog. Take a shower. Wash it off. I jog all the time, all that air in my lungs feels great, then I stand in the shower and it's freezing and I get out and just stand there, who needs a fucking towel, I'm trembling and dripping, I can feel myself sparkling in total control, clenching my fists and my face, every muscle so taut, clenching hard til I'm trembling, oh David you should stand there I swear you would tremble, oh David, David, ohhhhhhhhhhhhhhhhhhhhhhhhhhhhhhhhhhhhhhhh...

(Pause)

DAVID: Anyway, if you're not up for it—

KIM: So David. I was thinking. I need some help, planning a fund drive, for music in the schools. I wonder if you'd join me to help plan that.

DAVID: I'll let you know. Anyway, say hi to Carl.

KIM: You don't want to meet with me? Now?

DAVID: I probably shouldn't get into something like that right now. Thanks though.

KIM: But I mean, we could go to your house, and do the planning. Just the two of us. You know?

DAVID: Could we then have sex?

KIM: I have three daughters, you can't talk to me like that, it's disgusting, and a husband who needs me. I'd like to work with you David, 'cause you really are a good guy. I really like you, and I think you'd be great for the project that we were talking about, but you're going to have to promise me that you're not going to keep bringing up that other thing. Okay?

DAVID: You mean having sex?

KIM: That's it then, I'm going. I have things to do. Okay? So I'm going?

(KIM *goes.* DAVID *looks around.* SUSAN *enters.*)

SUSAN: Oh Sweety, I'm glad I caught you.

DAVID: How's it going with Peter Hanson?

SUSAN: He's so nervous. It's cute. He's waiting for me at the diner. Did you track down Kim Keeler?

DAVID: I did but she has things to do.

SUSAN: Well that's her loss. Anyway listen. I ran into Barbara Frank. She's got a D V D of Sam and Henry's softball team I'd love to show my sister. If you're going to the butcher could you pass by their place and pick it up?

DAVID: The Franks are way on the other side of the park.

SUSAN: I could get it late Friday but it would be really late since I'll be working late to make up for today.

DAVID: Well yeah okay, I'll swing by there.

SUSAN: You're the greatest. Hey there's Alice Molski. Why don't you ask her to have sex with you?

DAVID: She's hard to talk to, but I like her face. Okay.

SUSAN: If it works out, do you want the master bedroom?

DAVID: You guys can have it, we'll take Sam's room.

SUSAN: You're sure? It's a single bed. The room is so small.

DAVID: It'll be like college.

SUSAN: Leave the sheets in the laundry room afterward. I have to do a load today anyway so Sam has pants for tomorrow.

DAVID: What do you mean so Sam has pants for tomorrow? You got him three new pairs.

SUSAN: He won't wear them.

DAVID: He said that?

SUSAN: He left them in a heap outside his door.

DAVID: He picked them out, right?

SUSAN: He liked them at the store, but he doesn't like them now.

DAVID: He can't keep buying new clothes and deciding he doesn't like them.

SUSAN: If you know a way to make him wear them, go ahead.

DAVID: I'm not going to be able to have sex with someone I hardly know if there are three pairs of perfectly good pants in a heap in the hallway.

SUSAN: Don't get all distracted, honey. You've got to go have great sex with Alice Molski.

DAVID: I know.

SUSAN: You're not doing me a favor with this, right?

DAVID: Hey. I'm the one who brought it up in the first place.

SUSAN: I'm not going to enjoy it if the whole time I'm thinking you're just humoring me.

DAVID: Susan. Believe me. I want to have sex with someone else.

SUSAN: Oh there goes Alice, you better say something. And I better get back to Peter.

DAVID: Good luck there.

SUSAN: You too.

DAVID: Pork chops for dinner.

(SUSAN *goes.* ALICE *enters.*)

DAVID: Oh hi Alice.

ALICE: Hi David.

DAVID: So who does Annie have.

ALICE: She got Claire Johnson.

DAVID: Tessie was supposed to have Claire Johnson but everybody wanted her so she wound up with Miss Rhiner but she seems pretty good. Who does Evan have.

ALICE: We put him in the Hall School. They'll do better for his dyslexia.

DAVID: That's downtown right?

ALICE: David's shooting a documentary near there this fall. My David. So he can drop him off.

DAVID: Sam'll miss having Evan around but Hall is a good school. Hey I heard you got a promotion, weren't you already a partner?

ALICE: I got moved up in the pecking order.

DAVID: Susan was really impressed.

ALICE: Susan's firm is small so she can influence the way things operate, but my firm's huge so as I move up there are more of these big-name partners handing projects down to me that I may or may not want.

DAVID: Uh huh.

ALICE: And there's nobody I can pass things off to since the young lawyers are all busy trying to get through what they have to so they can move to some smaller firm where they'll have some real influence.

DAVID: Huh.

ALICE: And so even though I'm up near the top of this super-powerful international firm I'm basically stuck by myself every night until ten doing stuff no one else wants to do.

DAVID: Oh well. Say, do you want to have sex with me?

ALICE: That's really direct.

DAVID: We could go to my house.

ALICE: I have to tell you something. You know Arthur Denny? Jared's dad?

DAVID: I know who he is.

ALICE: Last spring I was watching Evan's softball game and Arthur came over and sat next to me on the grass and his knee touched my thigh and he left it there.

DAVID: Uh huh.

ALICE: It was one of those moments.

DAVID: Okay.

ALICE: Then during the third inning Jeremy Chang came over, you don't know him, his son goes to Sisters of Mercy, anyway he sat down on my other side and started talking to me, really enthusiastically.

DAVID: Uh huh.

ALICE: Arthur pulled back his knee and got quiet.

DAVID: He got quiet.

ALICE: Yeah.

DAVID: So—

ALICE: Then at the spring parent teacher dance when I was in line to get sushi Arthur came over and started making a point and he held my arm. Really firm. I could feel my pulse.

DAVID: Right.

ALICE: But just then Jeffrey Lamont, Mitchell's dad, pushed through the line and he bumped me.

DAVID: He bumped you.

ALICE: A real bump. My sushi bounced.

DAVID: Okay.

ALICE: Arthur disappeared.

DAVID: He disa—

ALICE: So I volunteered to chaperone for the field trip to the capitol but Arthur didn't chaperone, but you know who did?, Stacy Schatz's dad Howard.

DAVID: Howard Schatz.

ALICE: Howard rubs your shoulder when he talks to you, so he was going up and down the aisle rubbing the shoulders of all the moms.

DAVID: Uh huh.

ALICE: And when we pulled into the school I was getting off the bus and there was Arthur and his son asked my son if we wanted to go for ice cream.

DAVID: Huh.

ALICE: It was all coming together, you know? You hope and plan and then suddenly from nowhere...

DAVID: Right.

ALICE: But then Howard came down the steps and I leaned away fast as I could but he rubbed my shoulder right in front of Arthur and Arthur said it's too late for ice cream it's almost dinner and that was it, he was gone for the summer.

DAVID: I see.

ALICE: All summer I would pass by the school which was all closed up or walk across the empty baseball field.

DAVID: Gosh. So—

ALICE: So just now I dropped off Annie, I was coming down the hallway and there was Arthur coming in towards the stairs, he didn't see me or he was acting like he didn't so I looked to the side but there was Howard coming out of another kindergarten classroom and coming up behind me was Jeffrey Lamont and Jeremy Chang was there too, I have no idea why. The hall was packed with parents pressing against bodies that were pressing against mine. I didn't know where to look so I tucked my head down and forced my way through until I was back outside and there I was with nobody.

DAVID: I really would like to have sex with you, but if—

ALICE: That's the thing. Do I throw in the towel? I'm so sick of the games. But then you came along, right? You're really direct which makes it easy to let things out. It's so flattering, somebody who really goes out on a limb and makes the commitment, it's a great big pat on the back is what it is. So even though I'm feeling all these different things now and I'm not sure exactly where they'll land I have to tell you that someone accepting me for who I am goes a long way because I feel like with you it doesn't matter, you know? That I have a hangnail on my thumb. A little bit of hardened skin. So what. And a little scar from a sty that was removed two years ago under my eye. Who cares. Or that there's a crevice between two of my teeth that catches seeds or leafs or the casing from a bean, it doesn't matter, or that my back sweats, blotches of sweat drip down my back, big deal, I sweat, so what, or that when I'm talking to people I get this sense that something's hanging from my nose so I start touching my nose over and over and then the other person starts touching their nose and soon we're both touching our noses and no one's enjoying what anyone is saying so my back starts to sweat all the way down to the back of my thighs, I have very sweaty thighs and ankles and feet, so what, it doesn't matter that my legs sweat and my feet sweat or that I touch my nose a lot or that when other people are laughing I'm not laughing, they're looking at me to laugh and I want to be laughing but I'm not laughing I'm never laughing, I'm standing there picking my thumbs and licking my teeth and sucking on my saliva and my mucous and I'm sweating, my entire body is gushing until I stink up the room and that's fine.

(ALICE *starts off, gestures for* DAVID *to follow.*)

DAVID: I live this way.

(ALICE *heads off the other way,* DAVID *follows.*)

(*End of scene*)

Scene 2

(*The living room of* SUSAN *and* DAVID's *house.*)

(SUSAN *and* PETER *enter and sit.*)

PETER: But if we don't do it soon it'll be too late, I mean if we want them to be close in age, like your kids, which seems perfect.

SUSAN: I think only-children can be happy too.

PETER: Well yeah Chelsea likes getting all the attention and not having to share the cupcakes but I couldn't imagine not having my sister, even though she tortured me growing up, do your kids fight?

SUSAN: He picks on her now and then but she's starting to learn to hold her own.

PETER: So is two kids twice as much work or four times?, or I guess there's also a point where it cancels out, right?, when they can really play together or one kid takes care of the other?

SUSAN: They're just getting to the point where they can play together on Sunday mornings and let us sleep.

PETER: See we have to decide soon or we'll lose the playing-on-Sunday-mornings possibility though I guess we'll have the one-kid-taking-care-of-the-other thing but who wants to be so old you can't bend over, you know? Plus they say going back to the wiping and midnight feedings all over again is torture whereas if you do it again right away it's like you're still numb.

SUSAN: Well yeah.

PETER: We'll probably go for two, one is great though, whatever. Some people have three, you know?

SUSAN: I can't imagine that.

PETER: The kids outnumber you, right? So if they're fighting at the dinner table—

SUSAN: Or on a car ride—

PETER: Or if they're all doing homework at once—

SUSAN: I know.

PETER: Do you get three computers? And how the hell do you keep three computers running, do you need a full time tech person? Or if like two of them can have bottles but the third can't, or if two are toilet training at the same time, and somebody's always sick, right?

SUSAN: How do you take a day off to be with one of them when you know the other two are going to get sick later in the week?

PETER: They're always getting each other sick and getting you sick so before you know it you've got people vomiting in three bathrooms at once.

(Pause)

SUSAN: Would you like something to drink?

PETER: Sure.

(SUSAN *exits.*)

SUSAN: *(From off)* We have diet ginger ale, seltzer, and Coke.

PETER: I'll have Coke.

(Offstage: The sound of soda being poured.)

PETER: Nice house.

SUSAN: We like it.

(SUSAN *brings* PETER *a glass of Coke.* PETER *drinks.)*

PETER: So I guess you really lamp.

SUSAN: What?

PETER: Lamp. Lamp. Funny. My mind's stuck on lamp. I was going to say something and then I saw the lamp, it's a perfectly normal lamp, but for some reason I keep thinking lamp, and all I can think of is lamp. Lamp. Did that ever happen to you? It's funny how sitting and talking here feels so different from sitting and talking at the diner but it's exactly the same because with cell phones you're always reachable, even on a dark road in the middle of the wilderness you're never really cut off, but I guess the one major difference between here and the diner is at the diner if I screamed or grabbed you people would notice and discuss it and remember, it would count, but here if something happens and we don't say anything it's like it didn't happen, we're like the tree that falls and nobody noticed, this is the forest, I'm not even talking right now, I'm not waving this hand, I have no hands, I'm not here, nothing's here.

SUSAN: Do you want to go upstairs?

PETER: *(Finishes his drink, puts down the glass)* Let's go.

(PETER *stands, sinks to the floor.*)

PETER: Strange. One sec.

(PETER *gets back onto his feet, follows* SUSAN *off.*)

(DAVID *and* ALICE *enter.*)

ALICE: So what is it.

DAVID: What.

ALICE: You tell me.

DAVID: I don't know what you mean.

ALICE: Then I don't mean anything.

DAVID: Okay.

ALICE: But you did get quiet. Right? Please admit you got quiet.

DAVID: Okay.

ALICE: Do you want to tell me why?

DAVID: Sometimes I don't have much to say.

ALICE: You had a lot to say to Barbara Frank.

DAVID: Oh that's because she had the D V D of Sam's softball game. I didn't expect her to have it with her.

ALICE: You got really animated. You should have seen yourself.

DAVID: I thought I was going to have to go all the way to her house to get the D V D. They live way on the other side of the park. I didn't know when I'd get over there, so when we saw her and she just gave it to me, yeah I was excited.

ALICE: You were excited. All because she had this D V D.

DAVID: Susan's sister's coming this weekend and we really wanted to show it to her sister's kids. They've never seen him play softball.

ALICE: Uh huh.

DAVID: Should I not have taken the D V D?

ALICE: I can't tell you what not to do. But I can tell you, if I've invited someone to go somewhere, I don't walk a step ahead of them the entire way.

DAVID: I walked ahead of you?

ALICE: After you took the D V D from Barbara Frank. You walked ahead of me the whole way and got really quiet.

DAVID: I guess I was thinking about when would I go to the butcher.

ALICE: You were thinking about the butcher.

DAVID: Yeah, because I had been meaning to go to the butcher on my way to Barbara Frank's but now I didn't have to go there and I'm going to make pork chops tonight.

ALICE: Look. I told you about Arthur. And the others. Right?

DAVID: Uh huh.

ALICE: I need to know you're—ugh. This is hard. Ugh. I need to know you're really there. Ugh.

DAVID: I'm really here.

ALICE: Good.

DAVID: Do you want something to drink?

ALICE: Sure. What do you—

(ALICE *notices* PETER's *glass, picks it up, examines.*)

ALICE: You've had someone else over today? Of course you haven't. Never mind. (*Starts to sob, catches herself.*) You were saying.

DAVID: We have diet ginger ale, seltzer, and Coke.

ALICE: Where's the bathroom.

DAVID: There's one right down stairs.

(ALICE *goes.* DAVID *sits there.)*

(SUSAN *enters from upstairs.)*

SUSAN: Hey there, Babe.

DAVID: Hey honey. How are things going with Peter?

SUSAN: Moving right along. So was Alice interested?

DAVID: She's down in the bathroom.

SUSAN: That's so great, so we've got a full house.

DAVID: Sure do.

SUSAN: Say did you see Peter's glass by any chance?

DAVID: I guess that must be his.

SUSAN: He sent me for more Coke, I think as a stalling tactic. He keeps needing to be alone for a second to get centered or whatever.

DAVID: He's such a nice guy, Peter.

SUSAN: His nervousness is so sweet, I can't wait to make him feel really great and really comfort him all over.

DAVID: I'm really psyched about Alice too. She's complicated I have to say, but I think when we get going there's going to be all this passion and emotion and maybe even some tears all around.

SUSAN: Hey, one funny thing about Peter, you can't mention sex. He totally wants to have it, but if I say the word he gets all nutty.

DAVID: Kim really didn't like me talking about sex either now that you mention it. And with Alice, yeah she won't say anything about sex, she kind of talks around it.

SUSAN: It makes them feel self-conscious, doesn't it.

DAVID: It's like it's all right for their body to be doing it, as long as their brain doesn't find out.

SUSAN: Funny.

DAVID: I bet that's why Kim kept saying she wanted to come over as long as I didn't talk about sex. I didn't get the code.

SUSAN: Well you're good to go with Alice, right?

DAVID: Oh yeah, no complaints that's for sure.

SUSAN: I better get Peter his refill.

(SUSAN *exits to the kitchen.*)

DAVID: Oh I ran into Barbara Frank. She had the D V D with her. She'd just come from the video shop where they made copies.

SUSAN: *(Re-entering with glass filled with Coke)* Oh great, we'll definitely watch that this weekend.

DAVID: Have a great time with Peter.

SUSAN: You too.

(*The doorbell rings.*)

SUSAN: Could you get that?

DAVID: Sure thing.

(SUSAN *exits to upstairs.* DAVID *answers the door, lets in* KIM.)

KIM: I'm sorry David but I find it insanely ridiculous that kids in our day had choir and orchestra and band and jazz ensemble but our kids have a chorus led by a science teacher and that's it, so they'll never know that thrill of discovering music with their peers, you remember that total rush, right?, you're squishing your fingers into the holes and blowing til you're dizzy and there's spit flying everywhere and you're thinking this is stupid I can't believe they're making me do this and then suddenly my god you can't believe such

glorious music is really coming from you and these
friends you'll have forever. So the thing is I've found
a matching grant that can get us guitars, violins, a few
horns, a drum set, and someone to teach the kids and
enter them in festivals but we don't stand a chance,
it's slipping away, we're dead in the water unless we
can get major community support and now. I can't
do it on my own, David. I have tried and I have tried.
I need you to sit with me and brainstorm ideas, and
please hear me out because it's scary, I know. You
want a guarantee that it'll happen and you won't just
be sitting there in the dark but I'm telling you David
it's a mystery, it has to be, okay? I can't know just how
it'll go, we have to sit there and sweat it out, and to be
honest with you I can't imagine it, but I have to believe
there's a way to make that inconceivable leap, those
things happen in life, right? You can't see your way to
the next step but then you're suddenly there?, but it's
impossible to reason your way across that gulf David,
at some point you have to accept that it's out of your
hands and just trust that if we're good people and
what we're doing is deeply inspired and we just let go
with what we feel and go with our impulses we have
nothing to be afraid of so even though it seems like this
impossible ocean we can't turn our backs David we
really have to jump in and go for it because the stakes
are so high.

(ALICE *enters.*)

ALICE: Hi.

KIM: Hi.

ALICE: Kim.

KIM: Alice. Who does Evan have.

ALICE: We're sending him to Hall.

KIM: Oh the Hall School, that's terrific. How about Ann.

ALICE: Annie has Claire Johnson.

KIM: Belinda adored Claire Johnson, she's the absolute best.

ALICE: She seemed a little low energy.

KIM: Really.

ALICE: Yeah.

KIM: Oh.

DAVID: Anybody want something to drink?

KIM: I dropped by because I thought David might have some ideas about fundraising for music in the schools because of his work.

ALICE: We just got talking about one thing and another.

KIM: He's really good to talk to.

ALICE: Yeah.

DAVID: We've got diet ginger ale, seltzer—

(*Offstage: sound of footsteps.* ALICE, KIM, *and* DAVID *listen.* PETER *charges in holding an empty glass, not seeing the others, in a panicked state. He puts down the glass, closes his eyes, hugs himself and hunches over, shivering, writhes, staggers around, forces himself to stand up straight, breathes deeply, shakes out his arms, stops shivering, relaxes, loosens his clothing, touches himself sensually, opens his eyes, sees the others.*)

PETER: Oh hi hi, Kim, right? Your twins used to push my daughter on the springy horse on the playground.

KIM: Little Chelsea, they loved her.

PETER: Your girls were so great with her, do they baby sit?

ALICE: Your wife is Maxine, right?

PETER: Hi. Yes. We used to do food co-op on Sunday nights with you and David. Not this David, your David, how is he.

ALICE: He's good.

DAVID: Hey Peter.

PETER: Hey David, how's it going? Oh gosh.

KIM: So what brings you here then?

PETER: Oh yeah well, the thing is—*(laughs too loud)*

SUSAN: *(From off)* You okay down there?

PETER: *(To no one in particular)* Huh. So yeah.

(SUSAN enters.)

ALICE: Susan.

SUSAN: It's good to see everybody.

(In the following conversation, the slash / means that the next character begins her line as the first continues speaking.)

KIM: *(To SUSAN)* It's so great that Sam has Misses Bamara, she's great with reading / and she loves the Civil War.

SUSAN: *(To KIM)* We hear she isn't great with science but yeah / she's solid with reading.

ALICE: *(To SUSAN)* I'm sorry Tessie isn't in Claire Johnson's with Annie / it would have been fun.

SUSAN: *(To ALICE)* That would have been great but Miss Rhiner seems / terrific, she tries harder.

ALICE: *(To SUSAN)* Actually Claire Johnson seemed kind / of under the weather or something.

KIM: *(To ALICE)* You're going to love Claire Johnson, Belinda / adored her.

SUSAN: *(To KIM)* Belinda's in middle school, I can't believe / she's really moved on.

(DAVID *and* PETER *begin a separate conversation which occurs simultaneously.*)

KIM: *(To* SUSAN*)* The size of the middle school really worried us /but the diversity is the thing that we love.

DAVID: So did you guys get away at all?

SUSAN: *(To* KIM*)* It is big but yeah they say it's really diverse / which is an education in itself.

PETER: We spent a week in Nantucket.

ALICE: *(To* KIM*)* The size worried us but / yeah diversity is good.

SUSAN: *(To* ALICE*)* So who does Evan have?

DAVID: Sounds good.

ALICE: *(To* SUSAN*)* We're sending him to the Hall School / because he needs the extra attention.

KIM: *(To* ALICE*)* He'll get lots of attention there, / the student teacher ratio is great.

PETER: Did you guys get away?

ALICE: *(To* KIM*)* It's expensive but we figure this is the point where / he has to get what he needs.

DAVID: We went camping with some friends of Susan's.

SUSAN: *(To* ALICE*)* This is definitely the year, / *(To* KIM*)* oh and I forgot to ask about the twins.

PETER: Okay.

KIM: *(To* SUSAN*)* Nika has Mister McClellan and Rose has Jocelyn Phelps / about whom I know nothing.

ALICE: *(To* KIM*)* Mister McClellan, / congratulations.

SUSAN: *(To* KIM*)* Mister McClellan's the one / everybody wants.

KIM: We were lucky about that.

SUSAN: Definitely.

ALICE: Yeah.

(Pause)

DAVID: *(To* ALICE*)* So do you want to go upstairs?

ALICE: What?

DAVID: *(To* KIM*)* Alice was here first so I should go up with her.

ALICE: We can talk down here, right? All of us.

SUSAN: Go on up, Alice. It's okay.

ALICE: Me and David should go upstairs?

SUSAN: Peter and I'll be going back up in a minute.

PETER: You mean to check the walls some more?, to see if Maxine and I should paint Chelsea's bedroom the same color as Tessie's room? That's okay. I got a good look at the walls.

SUSAN: We didn't even start looking at the walls Peter, not really. Let's go on back up there and give the walls a really good look.

DAVID: Go upstairs, Peter. It's okay.

PETER: You're coming up too, right?

DAVID: I'll be up there in another room, with Alice.

PETER: I need some more Coke.

(PETER *exits to the kitchen, comes back with the whole two liter bottle of Coke, pours himself another glass, begins to drink it.*)

DAVID: *(To* ALICE*)* Let's head up then?

ALICE: Yeah, in a minute.

PETER: How about some Coke.

ALICE: Sure.

(PETER *pours* ALICE *some Coke. They drink.*)

KIM: While you guys are having your Coke, David and I should head upstairs to finish our talk about fundraising for music in the schools, if it really is okay with you Susan.

SUSAN: You and Alice should both go on up with David.

KIM: Both of us at once? Oh gosh, I don't think that would work, for Alice's sake really, because the stuff David and I have to get through is really specific and technical, for an outsider it would be totally dry.

ALICE: Maybe I should leave.

SUSAN: No.

DAVID: No.

KIM: Well if you're thinking along those lines...

ALICE: I could get some work done.

KIM: What a great feeling that is to be getting a jump on things, keeping a step ahead of your schedule, in total control. You'll wake up tomorrow on top of the world.

(ALICE *starts off.*)

ALICE: Oh well. Let's see, did I bring a jacket? *(She stops, returns to where she was standing before she started off.)* If anyone's going upstairs, I'm going upstairs.

DAVID: So how do I choose.

SUSAN: You take them both up there, honey.

KIM: I'm sorry to be a pain but I'm afraid if I don't have his total focus we'll just go around in circles and it'll be a big waste of everybody's time and I'd feel terrible.

SUSAN: You really don't have to worry about that because my husband is an amazing multi-tasker. He can explain the Viet Nam War to a three-year-old while driving through a blizzard, or handle an emergency call from a real estate agent while changing a really full pamper, or watch two movies on cable at the exact same time. He's got this ability to compartmentalize totally, keeping perfect track of two different things, moving back and forth so fast it's like he's in two places at once, he's all over everything until everything's all wrapped up.

DAVID: Wow. Thanks honey.

SUSAN: Somebody's got to blow your horn. So okay then?

KIM: I better have some Coke.

ALICE: More Coke for me.

PETER: More Coke.

(PETER *pours Coke. He,* ALICE, *and* KIM *drink.*)

DAVID: Shall we?

(*All head off together.* PETER *breaks away from the group, goes to the couch, sits, frozen. Pause*)

SUSAN: Are you o—

PETER: I can't do this.

(KIM *moves away from the others.*)

KIM: Neither can I.

(KIM *sits beside Peter on the couch. They talk to one another.*)

KIM: This is too weird for me, I'm sorry.

PETER: Everybody going into different rooms and shutting the door.

KIM: I was getting boxed into a corner.

PETER: Everyone knowing who's in there with who.

KIM: It was so fucking weird.

PETER: And then when you come out everybody's looking at you, and nobody's saying anything—

KIM & PETER: but they're thinking things...

KIM: And every time you see them for the rest of your life...

PETER: I know.

KIM: My god, this feels so much better, right? Being totally honest?

PETER: Yes.

KIM: It felt like I was about to crap in front of everybody there. Whew. My hands've stopped shaking, I can breathe again. Now we can just sit here, right in the open, and close our eyes.

PETER: Yes.

(KIM *leans on* PETER, *as* KIM *and* PETER *close their eyes, sit in silence.*)

DAVID: *(To* ALICE*)* So we can go upstairs just the two of us then.

ALICE: I really should, shouldn't I. But the couch looks good too. Ugh. I feel like I'm at the post office and I'm about to wind up in the wrong line. Let's see how it feels over there.

(ALICE *sits beside* PETER *on the couch.*)

ALICE: I don't know. Well, I guess yeah, upstairs sounds good.

(PETER *grabs* ALICE's *arm.*)

ALICE: *(gasps)*

PETER: I'm scared of being left alone with just one person. If I let go, will you please not go upstairs?

ALICE: Actually, don't let go.

(*They sit there,* PETER *gripping* ALICE's *arm.*)

SUSAN: If everybody's settling in down here for a bit I'll get us some snacks.

DAVID: Need help with that?

SUSAN: You go sit on the couch, honey.

DAVID: It looks kind of crowded.

SUSAN: You could squeeze in by Alice, no?

DAVID: You could squeeze in there too.

SUSAN: Well yeah, no I think I'll wait a bit.

DAVID: They're in this strange place all of a sudden, right? Sitting there like we're not even here? I wish they'd just come upstairs.

SUSAN: They feel safer this way, honey. Sometimes you have to take the cue from your guests. Let them come around in their own time.

DAVID: Yeah I guess. So what do I do now.

SUSAN: Keep an eye on everybody and let me know what I'm missing.

DAVID: Okey doke.

(SUSAN *exits to the kitchen.* DAVID *narrates what he sees for Susan.*)

DAVID: Well they're just sitting there. Nobody's doing anything. Peter's kinda resting, his eyes are closed

like he's having some kind of dream, maybe a bad
dream, something intense. Kim's eyes are closed too
but it's like she's seeing something right in front of her,
something kind of good I guess, she looks like she's in
a painting. Alice's eyes are opened, Peter's still holding
onto her but she's just staring right ahead, like a deer
in the headlights. Anyway I'm making pork chops
tonight, I need to get to the butcher so I can make us
a real special dinner. And I guess we should return
Sam's pants this weekend, but I'm not getting him any
new pairs unless he's really going to wear them. Oh
now Kim's taking her hand, she's drifting it up and
rubbing her hand on Peter's head, all across his head,
she's petting his head is what she's doing, she's petting
his head with her eyes closed and Peter's starting to
squirm, he's sorta squirming around and now Kim and
Peter are kind of pressing together, she's sorta drifted
up onto him, they're side to side but she's sorta on top
of him too and Alice is still there, still with that deer in
the headlights look, Peter's still squeezing her arm, and
now Peter's trying to get up, it's like he just thought
of something, he's got to be somewhere, but Kim's
hanging onto him, he's sorta drifting up and she's
hanging right on, digging her fingers into him, she's
not letting go no matter what and Peter's turned all
the way towards Alice, he's still gripping Alice's arm,
she's staring right at Peter, he's leaning in towards her
til he's right up against Alice, she's still staring up at
him, deer in the headlights, Peter's kind of pushing at
Kim, trying to scrape Kim away but she's pulling him
back and now he's spun around back to Kim, he let go
of Alice and Alice has sort of wrapped herself up and
hunched over, she's knocking herself against Peter's
back like a battering ram but Peter's grabbing Kim
with both hands and kinda shaking her and squeezing
her bones and yanking her up, their eyes are still closed
and Kim's grabbing the air, her fingers are like claws

and Peter's rubbing his face all over her, his mouth is
wide open, it's like he's breathing her or something,
they're breathing on each other and they don't look at
all happy about it, and now Alice is rubbing up against
Peter and clutching onto him like he's a buoy and
Peter's grabbing Kim but she's squirming and kicking
all of a sudden like she needs some breathing room but
Peter's wrapping his arms around Kim and Alice too
like he needs to yank himself up, and now somebody's
clothes just tore, they're tangled up and somebody's
biting somebody, Kim might be sobbing but she's
holding on tight, they're this great big animal that's
lurching around and squirming with their heads and
now it's climbing up, where's it going, I have no idea,
but it's climbing and climbing and sinking and sinking,
the great big animal is dropping down and now they're
on the floor, they're just lying there, yeah.

(During the above SUSAN *comes out with a tray of snacks,
watches.)*

*(*PETER, KIM, *and* ALICE *extricate themselves from one
another, crawl to different parts of the room, take out their
cell phones, push buttons.)*

PETER: Hi.

KIM: Hey Babe.

ALICE: Me.

KIM: Yeah.

ALICE: Mm.

PETER: Huh. Sure.

KIM: Hear your voice.

ALICE: Mm.

KIM: It is.

PETER: I know.

ALICE: Mm.

PETER: So proud.

ALICE: Yeah.

KIM: Has she called you?

PETER: When I pick her up.

ALICE: The check.

KIM: Yeah.

ALICE: I did.

PETER: Huh?

KIM: Lunch money.

PETER: Which dentist.

ALICE: Five thousand this month, five thousand in November.

KIM: We have to at her age.

PETER: What.

ALICE: We set that aside for the house.

PETER: I can't.

KIM: They all are.

ALICE: I'm not asking you to contribute.

PETER: The deductible.

KIM: I can't ask my parents.

ALICE: We discussed this.

KIM: But...

ALICE: When.

PETER: I said I could take her but not Tuesday.

KIM: I told you.

PETER: A job.

ALICE: Which one.

KIM: Fine I'll take them.

PETER: The prospectus.

ALICE: Then how—

KIM: Saturday.

PETER: Because I'm painting Tuesday morning. That's my work. It's what I do.

KIM: Somebody has to be home for the electrician.

ALICE: My conference.

PETER: What about what I said surprises you?

KIM: You what?

ALICE: The twenty-first to twenty-third.

KIM: That's supposed to be just the two of us.

PETER: Some flexibility on your part...

ALICE: I emailed you.

KIM: Because you said. To be home in time for—

PETER: Then reschedule.

ALICE: Seeing my mother.

KIM: Sunday.

PETER: But we're seeing them for Thanksgiving.

ALICE: He's going blind.

PETER: We are seeing them.

KIM: Last Sunday.

PETER: Thanksgiving.

ALICE: She's incapable of...

KIM: Last month.

ALICE: I can't.

PETER: We're seeing them for—

ALICE: Work.

KIM: The recital.

PETER: Thanksgiving.

ALICE: I have to.

KIM: Of course you didn't hear it.

PETER: You're never home before eight.

ALICE: Sunday night after ten.

KIM: What did I just say.

PETER: The cost of a sitter, for one thing.

ALICE: To go in late on a Monday?

PETER: You never do.

ALICE: It's not a question of—

KIM: I don't have to think of examples.

PETER: Never ever.

ALICE: Why do I open my—

KIM: Every time.

PETER: I always—

KIM: How can you—

PETER: No no no no no no.

KIM: Don't ever say that I—

ALICE: *(Prolongued grunt:)* Aaaaaaaaaaaaaaaaaaaaaaaaaa.

KIM: *(Deep breath, inhales, exhales)*

(Pause, all three listen.)

PETER: I know...

KIM: Babe.

ALICE: Yeah yeah.

PETER: I'm sor—

KIM: Fine.

ALICE: Yeah yeah.

PETER: I'm sor—

KIM: It is.

PETER: Fine.

ALICE: Okay.

KIM: Pick a night.

PETER: Sure I would.

ALICE: If I try a different pill.

PETER: I just get—

ALICE: I know.

KIM: Believe me.

PETER: Or to just go for a walk.

KIM: So do I.

ALICE: And I worry about...

KIM: The girls. The thing the doctor said. If the bumps keep bleeding.

PETER: Constantly.

ALICE: If he doesn't progress...

PETER: But yeah. Sure.

KIM: I know.

PETER: We really are.

ALICE: To keep that in perspective.

PETER: We are.

KIM: I know.

ALICE: He combed his hair.

PETER: When she gave me the hug.

KIM: Her cheek is all healed.

ALICE: She's pronouncing her "S"s.

KIM: Definitely. Friday night.

PETER: Me too.

ALICE: So do I.

KIM: Then next Friday.

PETER: Me too.

ALICE: So do I.

KIM: The Friday after that.

ALICE: Sounds good.

PETER: Me too.

ALICE: Mm.

KIM: One Friday next month.

ALICE: Right.

PETER: Bye.

(PETER, KIM, *and* ALICE *put away their cell phones, straighten themselves up, and face the group.*)

KIM: Bye bye Susan, this was great. David, we never did get to talk about the thing. See you Alice, good luck with Hall, say hi to David. Bye Peter, send us a card about your next show.

(KIM *goes.*)

ALICE: I'll see you all in the hallways. *(She goes.)*

PETER: Thanks for having me. *(He goes.)*

SUSAN: Well that was disappointing.

DAVID: When Kim showed up I should have told her I already had company, having the two women complicated everything.

SUSAN: Oh don't start blaming yourself now.

DAVID: And I should just have insisted everybody go upstairs. I know they would have, if I'd put my foot down.

SUSAN: You can't control other people, David. They want what they want and you have to accept that.

DAVID: They wanted to go up, and then they didn't want to go up, and even when they were on the couch they couldn't decide who wanted to be with who. They kept changing their minds about everything, it was so frustrating.

SUSAN: That's exactly right. We knew what we wanted, and we were direct about it, and if they wanted to play some kind of game, well next time we'll find people who're really ready to be with us.

DAVID: Next time?

SUSAN: This was only our first try.

DAVID: Yeah but...

SUSAN: You're not going to give up that easy, right? It takes time to find the right people. We have to shop around.

DAVID: But when will we ever have a chance like that again? When we're both free and the kids are out of the house, and everybody has totally unscheduled time, with no work, no birthday parties or vacations or soccer games or check-ups, when will that happen?

SUSAN: Do you want to go upstairs now, just you and me?

DAVID: We can't keep doing that.

SUSAN: I know.

DAVID: If we went up there now we'd lie down and close our eyes and imagine the people who were just here. The whole time we were touching each other we'd be thinking about their faces and their voices and their hands. I'm tired of you having to shut your eyes and imagine people, Susan. I want the people to be right here so you don't have to close your eyes to feel really good. And I want that for me too.

SUSAN: Oh honey.

DAVID: And I feel like the chances of that happening are getting less and less, like we might never get another chance like that and I messed it up.

SUSAN: You're putting way too much pressure on yourself, David. You have to be patient, okay? Because it really will happen for us, I know it.

DAVID: You think so?

SUSAN: Maybe when the kids are gone, and our parents aren't such a problem, or maybe sooner, maybe it'll be one day really soon when we're not even expecting it. We'll be walking in the park, after dinner, the sun'll just have started going down, and we'll be walking by the lake, and we'll see them, and they'll see us, and we'll go over to them, and we'll walk along with them, across the field, and we'll be thinking to ourselves we can't believe it, that it can be so natural, so perfect, and so incredibly easy. And before we even feel their new bodies against ours, before we feel their breath on our skin for the very first time, while we're still just walking along, with the red sunlight glowing all over us, we'll sort of stop, and they'll turn to us, and they'll take us in their arms, and they'll hold us, and they'll squeeze us, really hard, and we'll be free.

(There's a knock on the door.)

DAVID & SUSAN: Who's there.

(End of scene)

Scene 3

(The same living room. PETER *and* SUSAN *are seated.)*

PETER: They'll find him, they always do, but I have to leave my phone on if that's okay.

SUSAN: Of course it's okay.

PETER: If Dad would just try to escape through the front door like everybody else it wouldn't be a problem, the people who run the home are on the lookout for that, but he grabs Mom's glasses by mistake and just keeps on going not quite realizing he can't see til he winds up in some closet or corner of the basement.

SUSAN: Oh gosh.

PETER: And Mom's hysterical. Without her glasses she can't do her puzzles, she just sits there and screams.

SUSAN: Mm.

PETER: My sister and I trade off being on-call but her colonoscopy's this week so I have to be reachable.

SUSAN: It's so hard to adjust to a new place at their age. But they will.

PETER: I guess he'll resign himself and relax or lose it completely and stop caring. How are your folks.

SUSAN: My Mom's good, she's got this great husband. And my dad and his wife we moved into this communal thing, they live independently for now but they'll go across the yard into full-time care like your parents when it's time.

PETER: We wanted that for my folks but we missed the cut-off, they're past the caring-for-themselves point, so instead of starting independent and paying the flat fee they have to pay a huge sum every month for the duration.

SUSAN: But you like the place, right?

PETER: The facilities are great. The people are nice. It really is perfect for them.

SUSAN: So. This is our fifth first day of school. On the first one our girls were just starting kindergarten. Now they're in fourth grade.

(ALICE *enters from downstairs with her hand bag.*)

ALICE: I need two double "A" batteries.

SUSAN: Did you check the radio in the shower?

ALICE: Those are "D", I need double "A".

SUSAN: There's always *our* thing.

ALICE: I know. I just thought, in addition.

PETER: Should I run to the drug store?

ALICE: No. I'm just so pissed at David, my David. He said he was going for groceries so I put batteries on the list and crossed it off in my mind, but then he didn't go.

SUSAN: We have those little flashlights upstairs, I think they take double "A".

ALICE: If it works out, great.

PETER: I brought a cucumber. *(Pause)* I left it out of the fridge over night.

SUSAN: Good.

ALICE: Good. *(She takes hand lotion from her bag, squirts it on her hands.)*

PETER: Maxine uses that in the winter with the dry heat.

ALICE: Heat dries you out. Cold dries you out. Wind. Sun. Air.

(ALICE *offers the lotion to Susan, who squirts it onto her hands and offers it to Peter. All three squirt and rub it in without speaking.*)

(DAVID *and* KIM *enter from upstairs.*)

DAVID: Hey everybody.

PETER: Hey Kim. Hey David.

KIM: Hi there.

ALICE: Hi.

SUSAN: *(To* DAVID *and* KIM*)* Come say hi you two.

DAVID: We were just getting warmed up, so my back doesn't do like last time.

KIM: Or my knee.

DAVID: I put Sam's sheets in the hamper, right?

SUSAN: You took Kim in there?

KIM: Oh please, you should see the twins' room, or Belinda's floor, you can't walk on it.

DAVID: Don't be putting down our kids' favorite sitter.

PETER: Belinda baby sits?

ALICE: Is she liking Hamilton?

KIM: It's high school, you know, it's noisy but the teachers are great.

SUSAN: That's what we hear.

KIM: This year things start to really count for colleges and they have these great A P courses, she just called to let me know she got into A P Spanish.

(They sit there.)

PETER: You look good, Kim.

KIM: You look good too Peter. David too.

DAVID: Thanks.

PETER: Susan looks terrific as always.

SUSAN: Thank you, Peter.

DAVID: Alice looks especially good.

KIM: You do look good, Alice.

ALICE: Thanks.

PETER: You've got a kind of—

(PETER's *phone rings.*)

PETER: Hey. Oh thank you. Where was he. Good. Whose teeth. He has his own teeth. I don't know whose teeth those are, he has his own. In his mouth. Oh gosh. Could you show him? Put your hands in his mouth and pull. *(He hangs up.)* We moved my parents into a home.

KIM: As much trouble as they give you, you're lucky to have them.

SUSAN: You lost your mom this year, right Kim?

DAVID: We were sorry to hear that.

KIM: They're both gone now, and I'm telling all my friends to call your parents every day and tell them you love them.

PETER: For sure.

(Pause)

KIM: *(Taking out pamphlets)* Oh I brought these pamphlets from the art museum, so now we're seeing "the Power and Progress of Young Raphael".

DAVID: I have to remember that, when I run into Carl. I always say, "We had fun with your wife last week. At the museum."

SUSAN: It's too bad we have to keep secrets.

PETER: It's one of those things, yeah.

KIM: Like I tell the girls, if there are people you can't tell about your party to spare their feelings, that's okay.

SUSAN: Say honey, do we have double "A" batteries? Alice brought her thing.

DAVID: The little flashlights upstairs take double "A".

ALICE: If we like it, it'll be there.

PETER: I brought a cucumber. *(Pause)* I left it out of the fridge over night.

KIM: Good.

DAVID: Good. *(Pause)* So let's head up?

SUSAN: I think we should talk first, honey.

DAVID: We've been talking, honey.

SUSAN: But last time, at the end, I got a feeling people might want to talk about how things are going. Anybody?

(Pause)

KIM: You go first.

SUSAN: Well, just to get the ball rolling, somebody made the suggestion that we bring in other people.

PETER: Oh we couldn't.

ALICE: *(Shakes her head)* Mm.

KIM: I think I said something, but just in passing, I didn't mean we really should.

DAVID: You're sure?

KIM: Remember the first time, how long it took us to come around?

PETER: And if they don't come around, is the thing. We've kept this quiet.

SUSAN: Right.

ALICE: Plus, with the same people, you can let down your hair.

PETER: We have this promising thing. Sure there's work to be done. But let's work within it, to make it great.

SUSAN: In terms of working within it, out of the past four times, what have people liked?

DAVID: I liked the first time.

SUSAN: When everybody went away and came back?

DAVID: Yeah.

SUSAN: It was so awkward.

KIM: And messy.

DAVID: Yeah!

(Pause)

PETER: The next year was the one I really liked.

KIM: Me too.

SUSAN: We'd had some time to think about it.

PETER: But we weren't thinking.

SUSAN: Everybody just...

KIM: We were all going different directions.

PETER: But there was so much overlap.

KIM/SUSAN: Yes.

(Pause)

KIM: Then the third time, we had expectations.

SUSAN: It felt strained, right?

ALICE: I liked the third time. The music.

KIM: The music didn't do much for me.

PETER: Music can be distracting.

SUSAN: If they're singing about what you're doing.

KIM: Or violence.

DAVID: Or an octopus's garden.

(DAVID and PETER laugh, are quickly interrupted by:)

ALICE: *(As if in a trance)* But with the music, there were moments that were perfect. I wanted to die. I wanted to die. I wanted to tear off my skin and eat the sky and be dead.

PETER: We could try some music.

ALICE: Good.

(Pause)

DAVID: I guess one thing I was wondering is if we could limit the talking.

SUSAN: We can't keep people from talking, darling.

DAVID: Yeah but if we could keep it to certain breaks in the action.

KIM: I need to talk sometimes, I'm sorry. I'll try not to talk so much. Does everybody feel that way? Whatever. That's just how I am, I guess I get nervous. Well no, it's not just a nervous thing, it's a good thing, I start to feel good sometimes and I need to say something, that's me.

SUSAN: It's completely okay, Kim.

PETER: He didn't mean—

KIM: Oh god, now I'm silencing your criticism by being defensive, am I really ruining it for everybody?, I don't want to have to be on my guard the whole time for god sake shit, I'll try to keep quiet but sometimes I can't and it's not a bad thing, okay?, it's okay with everybody, right, if I need to say things now and then it's okay?

SUSAN: Of course it's okay.

DAVID: It's completely fine.

KIM: Good.

SUSAN: So.

ALICE: I wanted to mention, attentiveness.

PETER: But being attentive, that doesn't mean always stopping.

KIM: A pause isn't stopping.

SUSAN: Slowing down, can be good.

PETER: In the early stages, it's fine with me to be, meandering.

ALICE: Mm.

PETER: But there's a time for directness, right?

SUSAN: Sure.

PETER: And during that time, you can't just drop everything.

KIM: You mean like dozing off?

DAVID: Sorry about that.

ALICE: It's like my son's team. No one should be left alone under the basket waving their arms, shouting "I'm open I'm open".

DAVID: Can I just say something? On behalf of myself and Susan, we're really touched you could all be here.

(They exit to upstairs.)

(The front door opens. BELINDA and JONAH enter carrying back packs. They drop the back packs, head to the couch and make out furiously, gasping for breath. As they continue to make out: They rub their hands in one another's hair. They roll around, tumble to the floor, and roll back up onto the couch. They kick off their shoes. They rub each other over their clothes. They untuck and unbutton one another's shirts. They put their hands inside each other's clothes and rub. She wraps her legs around him as he lies on top of her.

*They grind their middles together, rocking. They start to
undo one another's pants. They stop kissing, still entwined.)*

BELINDA: What do you think?

JONAH: What do you think?

BELINDA: I think about the impact it could have. Will I
become obsessed. Will I lose all interest in my courses
and be unable to concentrate on homework and papers
and exams. Will it change the way I play piano. The
way I walk. The sound of my laugh. Will the hormones
in every corpuscle in my body be transformed so the
rhythm of my pulse changes and little hairs grow on
my forehead and I sweat at weird times and the pores
on my flesh give off a slightly different scent. Will my
friends avoid me. Will weird kids approach me. Will
you stop waiting for me between classes and holding
my hand in the cafeteria and leaning against me when
we walk down the hall.

JONAH: I guess I think more about the existential thing.
What really has meaning. My mother's screaming
about money feels unreal. But there's something
between you and me that's on a whole different plane.
It involves our bodies, but it moves beyond that. This
summer, we were apart for six weeks, but I could
stand in the woods and focus on sensations from the
relationship. The out of breath feeling of rushing to
get places. The frozen toes feeling from the walk when
we talked about Walden. The feeling of your tears on
my throat from the time you slammed the door on me
and came back out. I could summon that stuff, alone in
the weirdness of Vermont, and feel totally connected,
because we've generated this thing, spirit, or whatever.
It's like we're building a poem. And of course I want
to keep going further, of course it feels good in a
sensual sense, but I'm not being hedonistic in wanting

that pleasure, it's not greedy at all, because we're constructing something valid and real.

BELINDA: Wow.

JONAH: Yeah.

BELINDA: And this would be the perfect time, right? When else do they let us fill out a bunch of forms and go home?

JONAH: Only on the first day of school.

BELINDA: Plus we have this place.

JONAH: It is nice.

BELINDA: It's indoors. We don't have to roll around in the dirt and tree roots.

JONAH: Or deal with your dad checking in from his sound studio.

BELINDA: Or your mom listening through the walls of your apartment.

JONAH: You're sure the people you baby sit for aren't coming back?

BELINDA: They're at the art museum with Mom, I just called her. And if a neighbor saw us come in, I'm dropping off these D V Ds for the kids.

JONAH: So wow.

BELINDA: Yeah. Mmm.

(They resume kissing, start to take off their pants, stop suddenly when—)

(DAVID hurries on from upstairs, disheveled, unbuttoned, and shoeless. Belinda and Jonah freeze, using the couch to hide themselves.)

DAVID: *(To off)* There should always be band-aids upstairs.

SUSAN: *(From off)* Tessa used them for her project.

DAVID: *(Exiting to downstairs)* We shouldn't have to go to the basement to get band-aids.

SUSAN: *(From off)* She left them in the kitchen.

DAVID: *(From off)* I can't hear you, I'm in the basement.

(SUSAN hurries on from upstairs, disheveled, unbuttoned, and shoeless.)

SUSAN: *(To off)* The band-aids are in the kitchen.

(SUSAN exits to the kitchen, as DAVID enters from the basement with an empty band-aid box.)

DAVID: *(To off)* If the box is empty you shouldn't put it back.

SUSAN: *(Off)* I'm not talking about the empty box, there's a big full box of band-aids, I saw it in here by the magazines, or with the bottles. Could you check the living room?

DAVID: *(To off)* One second. My back. *(He leans back against a wall.)*

SUSAN: *(Off)* You didn't warm up enough.

DAVID: *(To off)* We started off way too fast, everybody was too charged up, and why do they have to keep it so dark, I don't care what bulges or lines anybody has, I need to see what the hell's going on.

SUSAN: *(Off)* Don't get negative now honey, don't even go there, we're the hosts, we have to deal with what happened and just keep going.

(KIM hurries on, disheveled, unbuttoned, and shoeless, holding her eye, as she heads to the kitchen.)

KIM: I need an ice cube, when Peter got cut we bumped heads.

DAVID: Gosh Kim.

SUSAN: *(coming out with a box of band-aids, to* KIM*)* I've got to get Peter these band-aids, can we get you some Advil?

KIM: *(Heading into the kitchen)* My stomach can't take Advil, do you have Tylenol?

SUSAN: *(To* DAVID*)* In the hutch, in the little basket.

DAVID: The little basket...

SUSAN: *(Handing* DAVID *the band-aids)* I'll get the Tylenol, you give these to Peter.

(As SUSAN *exits to the kitchen,* PETER *hurries on from upstairs, disheveled, unbuttoned, shoeless, pressing a towel to the side of his stomach.)*

PETER: Never mind the band-aids, the cut was long but it wasn't deep, I'm just sorry about bloodying-up your towel, but I was wondering if I could get some ice for the top of my head, it's swelling up.

DAVID: One ice cube, sure. *(Exiting to the kitchen)* So you got cut by Alice's ring?

PETER: *(To off)* It was my fault, Alice expected me to go one way but I can't put weight on my left shoulder so I went the other way.

DAVID: *(From off)* How'd you hurt your shoulder?

PETER: *(To off)* Lifting the bikes. *(To himself)* Or playing badminton.

*(DAVID *comes out with an ice cube for* PETER.)*

DAVID: Would some Advil help?

SUSAN: *(Off)* Advil, I got it.

PETER: *(To off)* Any chance you have Bufferin? Or how about Excedrin, I could use the caffeine.

SUSAN: *(Off)* We might have Excedrin.

(KIM *comes out from the kitchen pressing an ice cube to her head.*)

KIM: Oh Peter it's my fault we bumped heads, I should have backed off but I'm being careful with my neck.

PETER: What happened to your neck?

KIM: I get this shooting pain. I should see somebody.

ALICE: (*Off*) Shit.

(SUSAN *hurries out from the kitchen carrying a tray with jars of pills and two glasses of water to see:*)

(ALICE *enters from upstairs, disheveled, unbuttoned, and shoeless, carrying her purse. She walks extremely slowly, one cautious step at a time, arms extended for balance, looking straight ahead at all times.*)

ALICE: Bouncing. Everything. This happens. When I. Jerk around.

SUSAN: Do you want a Dramamine?

ALICE: Pill. In my bag. Here.

(DAVID *takes the bag from* ALICE, *goes through it.*)

ALICE: Little bottle. With a long name.

DAVID: Loraz–epp—

ALICE: No.

DAVID: Aceta–minnow—

ALICE: No.

DAVID: Modaffff—

ALICE: No.

DAVID: Guy-nuh-—

ALICE: No.

DAVID: Lex-up—

ALICE: No.

DAVID: Immodal-die-pyri-—

ALICE: Yes.

(DAVID *struggles to open the jar.*)

ALICE: Never mind. It's passing. Okay.

(ALICE *lets down her arms, relaxes.*)

ALICE: I better sit.

(DAVID, SUSAN, PETER, *and* KIM *escort* ALICE *to the couch, where they see* BELINDA *and* JONAH. *All characters except for Jonah begin a 5-part Simultaneous Babbling, in which certain* EMPHASIZED WORDS *are spoken more loudly. During the Simultaneous Babbling, all straighten their clothes and hair as nonchalantly as possible. The 5 simultaneously babbled parts are:*)

(#1. PETER)

PETER: *(To* BELINDA*)* Oh Belinda Belinda, you're at Hamilton, I think you know this girl who sits for my daughter, her name is SALINA, SALINA KUBICEK she goes to Hamilton, SALINA KUBICEK is her name and she goes to Hamilton, I'm so impressed that you got in there, we're hoping for my daughter to go there someday, it's so great that the public high school can be so terrific, it's great that it's public because of the DIVERSITY, it's such a terrific thing to be going to school with people of all different backgrounds, plus are you happy with the FACULTY?, we hear it's terrific, right?, the faculty and they say that the GUIDANCE COUNSELORS make all the difference because of the attention you get which they say really matters for colleges, that they can write you recommendations and oh right I saw you in the middle school CHRISTMAS CONCERT a couple years back, we went to see the son of a friend of ours but I remember you were playing piano that was really terrific, it was a really great concert and you were terrific that was fun, it was a great great concert that must have been fun it really was good, we sure enjoyed that concert.

(#2. ALICE)

ALICE: *(To* BELINDA*)* You're Kim's daughter Belinda, right?, that's great that you got into Hamilton. I want my kids to go there because of the ATTENTION they give you, right? Are you happy so far? We hear the teachers are good but the main thing is that the GUIDANCE COUNSELORS really know who you are, it's a big school but you're not a number, the GUIDANCE COUNSELORS really keep an eye on you and when it's time for college they can write you recommendations because they know who you are. There's a boy CODY FOWLER who goes there, CODY FOWLER is his name and he interns at my husband's production company, and he says they give you a lot of homework but that seems to be the case wherever you go nowadays but he likes it and he says everybody likes it. I saw you in the CHRISTMAS CONCERT because Annie was looking at middle schools and we weren't sure but that concert was so much fun that's what swayed us and you were playing piano for the choir, you were really good that was good, that was a lot of fun, I definitely remember you at that concert, you played piano, that was fun.

(#3. KIM)

KIM: *(To* BELINDA*)* Oh Belinda Belinda, *(To* ALICE*)* this is my daughter Belinda *(To* BELINDA*)* this is Alice Molski, your sisters know her son Evan. *(To* ALICE*)* We do love Hamilton because you're not a number. *(To* PETER*)* Your sitter goes to Hamilton? *(To* BELINDA*)*

Do you know SALINA KUBICEK sweety? You don't
know SALINA KUBICEK? Do you know who SALINA
KUBICEK is? She goes to Hamilton. *(To Susan and*
DAVID*)* We looked at all the schools and some of
them were smaller or experimental and even a couple
private schools but I didn't get the feeling that the
education was any better, *(To Alice and* PETER*)* and
gradually we realized that yes Hamilton is big but
they have a great EDUCATIONAL PHILOSOPHY,
they really include the parents—*(To* BELINDA*)* Do you
know CODY, CODY FOWLER, do you know him? *(To*
SUSAN*)* They include the parents and they have a great
philosophy—*(To* BELINDA*)* Do you know a MAYA
FRANK? David and Susan are asking about MAYA
FRANK, sweety? She goes to Hamilton. *(To* PETER*)*
Oh right the CHRISTMAS CONCERT. *(To* BELINDA*)*
Remember that Christmas concert sweety? *(To Susan,*
Alice, PETER*)* She played piano for the chorus, that was
fun, she really enjoyed that, she loves playing piano
but playing for the chorus was a special thrill, they
got to travel but that concert was the best, wasn't that
a great concert, oh that was fun, it was a Christmas
concert, that was fun.

(#4. DAVID *and* SUSAN*)*

SUSAN: Oh Belinda, hi there.

DAVID: Belinda hey.

*(*DAVID *and* SUSAN *observe the others without speaking,*
until KIM *addresses them, at which point they join in.)*

SUSAN: *(To* KIM*)* Well sure, we like what we hear about
Hamilton, / it would be great if Sam could go there.

DAVID: *(To* KIM*)* It really is a great place, that's what /
everybody says it's really the place to go.

SUSAN: *(To* DAVID*)* I really like the way they INVOLVE THE PARENTS / in everything, that has to help, the involvement.

DAVID: *(To* SUSAN*)* They really INVOLVE THE PARENTS / that seems to be the consensus.

SUSAN: *(To* BELINDA*)* Oh our friend's daughter, *(To* DAVID*)* What's the Frank girl's name?

DAVID: *(To* SUSAN*)* The Frank girl? Oh Maya.

SUSAN: *(To* DAVID*)* MAYA FRANK, that's right. *(To* BELINDA*)* Do you know MAYA FRANK?

DAVID: *(To* BELINDA*)* Hey we saw you in that concert a few years back, that really was good.

SUSAN: *(To* BELINDA*)* That was a great concert, you were playing piano for the chorus / it was a CHRISTMAS CONCERT and you were playing piano, that really was fun, it was a great great time for everybody, yeah it was.

DAVID: *(To* BELINDA*)* I really enjoyed that concert, it captured the holiday spirit all right, it really was a good time, it was a whole lot of fun it really was, and you were playing the piano that really was good.

(#5. BELINDA*)*

BELINDA: *(To* KIM*)* Mom oh mom. *(To* PETER*)* Yeah I go to Hamilton. *(To David and* SUSAN*)* Hi there. Hi. *(To* ALICE*)* Yeah, I guess I like Hamilton. *(To* PETER*)* I don't think I know any Salina Kubicek. It's a pretty big school. If she's not in tenth grade I probably don't know her. *(To* KIM*)* I don't think I know her. If she's not in the tenth grade I probably don't know her. *(To* ALICE*)* Yeah the guidance counselors are good. You get a lot of attention. *(To* PETER*)* You should have your daughter go there. I'm pretty glad I got in. *(To* KIM*)*

Salina Kubicek must be not in my grade. *(To* ALICE*)* I
know that name, Cody Fowler. I don't know. The name
sounds familiar. Maybe I know Cody Fowler. *(To* KIM*)*
It's a big school. I'm not sure. *(To* SUSAN *and* DAVID*)* I
know Maya Frank. Yeah. I know Maya Frank. She goes
to Hamilton. She was in my class last year. I know her,
yeah. *(To the others, alternately)* Yeah, that was a fun
concert. That was me. I played piano. That was fun. I
miss that. That was a good chorus. That was a good
experience. I played piano. That was good. Thanks.
Thanks. That was good. That was good. Yeah.

(The 5-part simultaneous babbling peters out. Pause)

BELINDA: *(To* DAVID *and* SUSAN*)* Anyway I'm so so
sorry for letting myself in without telling you guys
but the thing is they let upperclassmen go early on
the first day of school, *(To* KIM*)* they have us sign all
these forms and then we're free, *(To* DAVID *and* SUSAN*)*
so I thought I'd drop off these D V Ds for your kids,
(To KIM*)* remember Mom we were saying all the old
Disney and that stuff sits on the shelf but Sam and
Tessa would love them *(To* DAVID *and* SUSAN*)* and I
didn't want to leave them on the stoop so I hope it's
okay that we came in and took a second to relax from
the walk or whatever but we're on our way out now,
this is Jonah.

DAVID: Hey Jonah.

SUSAN: Hi there.

JONAH: Hi.

BELINDA: Anyway Jonah's going to help me study for
the P S A Ts, he did amazing, he's a junior, so we're
going to the public library and this was right on the
way pretty much and I know I'm only supposed to
use the keys to your house when I'm bringing the kids
home from school but that one time we had a hand-
me-down coat for Tessa you did say I could let myself

in to drop it off so I thought this would be in the realm of all right and I'm so so sorry I didn't ring the bell but I was sure you guys were at the museum like my Mom said.

KIM: We're *going* to the museum is what I meant, we're on our way out now, we just decided to stop here to catch up for a bit but please don't tell your father, he doesn't care for museums but if he heard we came back here without inviting him that would hurt his feelings so you can't say a word because the thing is we're planning a surprise party for his birthday if you must know, it's not til March but it's a big one, he's been all worried about turning the big five-two so we wanted to do something really special and he absolutely can't have a clue or the surprise would be totally ruined, that's why I asked these people who aren't so close with your dad to help plan it, if I chose Daryl and Beth or the Milligans you know they'd give it away but my museum friends never see your dad so they're perfect for the mission which we've been totally enjoying, we just kicked off our shoes and let loose and bumped heads because we were rehearsing this skit if you must know, we worked up a skit that involves running and bumping and ice cubes and band-aids, all that skit kind of stuff, your dad'll laugh his head off, but when March rolls around if we finally decide not to do the skit because of scheduling or something you still can't say a word about it ever to anyone because we'll definitely use it another year and it's really so great, should we show it?, just a peek?, just a bit?, no we really really can't, because we're off to the museum, let's go.

SUSAN: Okay, we'll head out then.

DAVID: I'll round up the shoes.

KIM: *(To* BELINDA*)* We can drop you guys off on the way.

PETER: Wait, we can't go yet, because...

ALICE: Yeah.

PETER: We haven't finished the thing.

ALICE: Really.

KIM: It's so hard to tear ourselves away from working on the skit but—

*(*PETER *and* ALICE *close in on* KIM.*)*

PETER: I just had this great idea for the skit and I'm dying to go back up and show you my idea.

KIM: We are a museum group after all. Did you bring your car, Alice?

PETER: I'm just shaking you, just gently, I'm not angry.

ALICE: I'm sorry to hold you by the hair but you can't just change the plan like I'm not here, I'm here.

KIM: My car can fit you all if we squeeze.

*(*KIM *tries to go,* PETER *and* ALICE *pull her back, these three struggle, it becomes tender, they embrace.)*

KIM: Yes the skit. We can't stop now. What was I thinking.

PETER: Let's go upstairs then.

ALICE: Yeah.

*(*PETER *and* ALICE *run upstairs.)*

KIM: *(To* BELINDA*)* You guys can walk to the library, right? *(To* JONAH*)* Thanks for helping her study. *(To* BELINDA*)* I can't wait to see you at dinner and hear all about your day. *(She runs upstairs.)*

DAVID: *(To* BELINDA*)* Say that was really sweet of you guys to drop off the D V Ds.

SUSAN: The kids'll really enjoy those.

BELINDA: Actually I was wondering if before we go I could take Jonah downstairs to show him one of the movies. Not the whole thing, just one part. You can go up. We'll be really quiet. We won't be long. We'll let ourselves out.

SUSAN: Well

DAVID: I...

JONAH: *(To* DAVID *and* SUSAN*)* You know how it is, right?, when there's this scene in a movie you loved since you were three? It might be stupid to everybody else but for you it really resonates, it's got all these associations from childhood or whatever, and as you go through the different stages in your life you're always comparing it to stuff, finding references to it everywhere, it's all wrapped up in how your brain works but it's totally private, it's all within yourself, this thing that's so rich and powerful and perfect to you means nothing to anyone else. And then one day you find someone you think might totally get it and you can't wait to show them to see if finally for the first time in your life you're not alone.

SUSAN: Okay.

*(*JONAH *and* BELINDA *exit downstairs.* BELINDA *comes right back out.)*

BELINDA: If you guys get done early don't let Mom go home yet? When we stopped by there just now Dad was there with these friends of hers, they're planning her a surprise party, she really can't know they're there.

SUSAN: Okay, dear.

*(*BELINDA *exits downstairs.)*

DAVID: So we can't tell Kim what's going on at her place.

SUSAN: That's right.

DAVID: I guess we shouldn't say anything to Kim about what's going on downstairs either.

SUSAN: We probably shouldn't.

DAVID: And we can't tell the kids downstairs what's going on upstairs.

SUSAN: Nobody wants to know what anybody else is doing, honey. They're all happy doing their thing.

DAVID: They're amazing.

SUSAN: What do you mean?

DAVID: They make up incredible stories on the spot, saying just the right thing so they can slip right on by, and they just keep on going full speed ahead, nothing can stop them.

SUSAN: They do have a lot of energy. And a way with words.

DAVID: Not me. I can't keep up. All the rules for when to say what to who and how to cover up this while trying to do that. There's no more space in my brain and I'm tired.

SUSAN: You want to stop having sex with other people?

DAVID: Yeah, I think I do. How about you?

SUSAN: I could let it go. It was a nice tradition for a few years. It lasted a lot longer than our reading group. Are you okay?

DAVID: When we were upstairs I saw you doing that thing with your fingers.

SUSAN: (Squeezing her fingers) It's just a tingling, and then they get cold, it doesn't really hurt it's just weird.

DAVID: When will you get the results.

SUSAN: Tuesday. It's probably nothing, honey.

DAVID: I know.

SUSAN: You were really counting on today to lift your spirits, weren't you.

DAVID: Yeah I guess, with mom going down hill so fast, and things piling up again at work. And the kids aren't coming home for dinner?

SUSAN: Sam wanted to go out with his gang, he hasn't seen them all summer, so when Tessie asked if she could eat at Allie's what could I say?

DAVID: I know, but it would be nice if they ate with us on the first day of school.

SUSAN: I agree.

(Sounds of sex from above.)

(Sounds of sex from below.)

DAVID: Well I want to do *something*.

SUSAN: I had an idea. But I don't know how you feel about it.

DAVID: What.

SUSAN: When I saw the pamphlet from the art museum, I had this daydream. I saw us all looking at the painting of those beautiful naked bodies floating up into the clouds. But the thing is, the bodies in the painting were ours. We thought we were looking at other people, but we were looking at ourselves. We were naked and gorgeous and swirling up into the clouds, and we didn't have to lie or hide or pretend, it was the absolute beautiful truth.

DAVID: So you want to go to the art museum?

SUSAN: I do.

DAVID: It won't be like in your daydream, you know. Chances are we'll just be standing there looking at a bunch of paintings.

SUSAN: Well it's always a risk now isn't it.

DAVID: Okay.

SUSAN: We can?

DAVID: Sure. I'll go get our shoes.

SUSAN: First, come here.

(DAVID *and* SUSAN *embrace.*)

(*Sounds of sex from above and below.* DAVID *and* SUSAN *stand there embracing.*)

END OF PLAY